COLLEGE BASKETBALL: YOU are the COACH

Nate Aaseng

 Lerner Publications Company ▪ Minneapolis

To Bill and Dave Jansen
and other dedicated students
of the game

Copyright © 1984 by Lerner Publications Company

All rights reserved. International copyright secured. No part of this book may be reproduced in any form whatsoever without permission in writing from the publisher except for the inclusion of brief quotations in an acknowledged review.

Manufactured in the United States of America

LIBRARY OF CONGRESS CATALOGING IN PUBLICATION DATA

Aaseng, Nathan.
 College basketball—you are the coach.

 Summary: The reader is invited to make coaching decisions for ten crucial situations in NCAA tournament games. Presents the coaches' actual decisions and their results.
 1. Basketball—Coaching—Juvenile literature.
 2. National Collegiate Athletic Association—Juvenile literature. [1. Basketball—Coaching] I. Title.
 GV885.3.A19   1984   796.32′3′077   83-19996
 ISBN 0-8225-1555-5 (lib. bdg.)

2 3 4 5 6 7 8 9 10 93 92 91 90 89 88 87 86 85

CONTENTS

Become the Coach!   5

1 A Tall Order for a Short Team   7

2 Choose Your Desperation Shot   18

3 The Unstoppable Elgin Baylor   26

4 The Dangers of Playing It Safe   36

5 Workhorses vs. Greyhounds   46

6 Off to Beat the Wizard   56

7 Taking the Gola Challenge   66

8 Senior Honors   74

9 Axing Carolina's Tall Timber   82

10 The Phi Slamma Jamma Talent Show   92

Become the Coach!

You're about to get a close-up look at the showcase event of college sports, the National Collegiate Athletic Association's basketball tournament. Each year the final four teams in the tournament provide such gripping entertainment that tickets to their matches are nearly impossible to get. You won't need a ticket to any of these events, however, because you're not going there as a spectator. You are the coach of ten different final-four teams.

Have you ever wondered why college coaches seem like such an excitable lot? Many of them pace the sidelines, mangle programs in their sweaty palms, leap out of their seats countless times per game, and scream at players and officials. You'll soon find out why they are so edgy. The pressure really mounts when you face such situations as

- stopping a player who has a nine-inch height advantage over your center
- scoring a tie-breaking basket in the last three seconds of a game
- protecting a one-point lead

Some tremendous athletes will be out to challenge your wits and your courage. Lew Alcindor (now known as Kareem Abdul-Jabbar), Elgin Baylor, Bill Walton, and Marques Johnson are a few of the talented stars you must beat. Defending national champs from UCLA and LaSalle top the list of teams standing in the way of your title dreams.

These ten championship games from 1956 to 1983 prove that there are few easy answers and no pat formulas for winning. The same strategy, used twice, may work one time and fail the next. As coach, you will have to probe the scouting reports for clues about your opponents' strengths and weaknesses that can help you succeed. You must steer your team away from any glaring mismatches that your opponent will exploit.

These ten games also show that there is a way to beat every kind of team. Hot shooters, speedsters, great rebounders, tall teams, and even those with a large edge in talent can be overcome with some strategy and effort. Of course, you will also find that coaches are dealing with human beings, and that means unexpected thrills, disappointments, and magic moments.

Get ready to enter a packed arena. In it there is a large bloc of fans and a roster of players who are hoping desperately for the thrill of their lives, an NCAA crown. You won't disappoint them, will you, coach?

1 A Tall Order for a Short Team

Lew Alcindor

You are coaching the Drake University Bulldogs.

The NCAA championship basketball tournament has become, in the words of one coach, a "UCLA bullfight." One by one, teams come out to challenge the UCLA Bruins, who toy with them a while to provide some excitement before slaughtering them. This year, it's your turn to face them.

These particular UCLA stars, coached by John Wooden, have won two straight NCAA titles going into this 1969 tournament. In each of these three years, the toughest question for teams facing UCLA has been, "How do you stop Lew Alcindor?" No one has yet found a good solution.

7

Now you face the same question. You must come up with a defense against the Bruins' 7-foot, 2-inch center in this semifinal match. The task is going to be even more difficult for you than for most teams because there isn't a player in your starting lineup who can even see over big Lew's shoulder. How can your unusually short team possibly compete with such a dominant big man?

Look at Alcindor's record.

Lew Alcindor's three-year record at UCLA is 86 wins and 2 losses. Both defeats were two-point losses, and one of them came when Alcindor was bothered by an eye injury. Lew was so far beyond other players that he led the UCLA freshmen to a win over the UCLA varsity back in 1966, when the varsity players were the defending national champs!

In his first official game as a Bruin, Alcindor scored 56 points, and he has gone on to score over 2,200 more in his three-year career with UCLA. This season he has led UCLA to a 27-1 record, with an <u>average</u> victory margin of over 20 points!

With exceptional coordination to match his height, Lew can flip hook shots into the basket without a chance of their being blocked by even his tallest opponents. As his 63.9% shooting accuracy shows, Alcindor doesn't miss often. He also soars above the court for rebounds and destroys opponents' confidence by blocking their shots.

UCLA's Lew Alcindor is a giant-sized problem, especially for Drake.

To make matters worse for you, UCLA's offense is more than a one-man show.

With all the attention that Alcindor gets, it's easy to overlook the fact that the Bruins are loaded with talent. This game's lineup will include sharpshooters John Vallely and Lynn Shackelford, defensive standout Kenny Heitz, and an impressive pair of sophomore forwards, Curtis Rowe and Sidney Wicks. Any of these players is capable of scoring if you concentrate too much on stopping Lew.

The Bruins have avoided the mistake of letting Lew do it all. They like to create scoring chances with an attacking fullcourt press. Opponents find it difficult to throw the ball inbounds as the Bruins chase them all over the court. This tactic has often unnerved teams who were already wary of facing the mighty Bruins. The most recent example of this strategy is the 90-52 drubbing that UCLA gave to highly rated, once-beaten Santa Clara.

Curtis Rowe

Jump-shooting John Vallely has a marksman's accuracy from the outside.

Your Bulldogs are an exciting veteran team, but they're awfully short.

Not many teams can compete at the championship level without a solid big man, but you'll have to struggle without one. The best you can do for a center is 6-foot, 5-inch Al Williams, who will be at a nine-inch disadvantage against Alcindor. Reserve center Gary Odom, at 6 feet, 8 inches, could add some height. He played well and scored 10 points against Colorado State in your most recent win.

You do have a team full of deadly shooters who have carried you to a 24-4 mark this season. Most of these players have been starting at the college level for years and are not frightened by UCLA's reputation.

The key man in your attack has been 6-foot, 3-inch guard Willie McCarter. One of your most effective tactics has been to clear space on the court for Willie to work one-on-one against another guard. Few college players can stay with him in that situation, as he showed in a 21-point effort against Colorado State.

Forward Willie Wise and reserve guard Gary Zeller also own excellent shooting touches, and forward Dolph Pulliam has won raves for his defensive work.

Your Bulldogs like a fast-paced game on both offense and defense. The "belly button" man-to-man defense that they use accurately describes how closely they guard their opponents. With good bench strength to help you keep fresh players in the game, your super-quick team likes to turn the game of basketball into a series of foot races.

The experts, however, claim that this kind of fast-paced game won't work against UCLA. They believe that a patient, slow-paced game and a tight zone defense is the only way to beat the Bruins.

What's Your Decision?

You are the coach.
Your team is a 13-point underdog against UCLA.
What strategy will you use to give your Bulldogs a fighting chance against the taller Bruins and their star center?

#1 Slow the offense to a crawl to keep the ball away from the Bruins.

#2 Fall back into a tight zone defense that clogs the middle.

#3 Get more height into your starting lineup by starting Odom in place of Williams.

#4 Play your usual belly button man-for-man defense with Williams guarding Alcindor.

Choose your strategy. Then turn the page to find out which strategy the Drake coach used.

Drake chose option #4.

At first glance it seemed insane to try and cover the great Alcindor with a man nine inches shorter. But Drake coach Maury John reasoned that quickness was his team's main strength. If his players could swarm around the other four Bruins, they might force mistakes before the ball ever got to the star center.

A fast-paced team such as Drake would probably feel awkward with any kind of slowdown game (#1). Zone defenses that clog the middle (#2) are not always effective against a team with good outside shooters, and nearly every one of the UCLA starters can shoot the netting off the basket. It might be nice to add some height against the UCLA giant, but three inches isn't going to help much (#3). Nobody is going to block Alcindor's shot anyway, and the only way to keep him from reaching rebounds is to block him out with the body.

Here's What Happened!

Drake's strategy failed to keep UCLA from breaking into an early, 10-point lead. The Bruins were able to work the ball in to Alcindor, and the Bulldogs were fouling right and left in a futile attempt to keep him from scoring. Midway through the first half, UCLA led 29-19 as Drake committed six fouls against Alcindor. But thanks to a rare error by UCLA coach John Wooden, the Bulldogs got back into the game. While on the verge of breaking open the game, Wooden chose to give his starters a rest. No sooner had they sat down than the Bulldogs pounced on the reserves to close the gap to 29-25.

The Bruin starters hurried back into the game, but they were unable to shake the Bulldogs. Under pressure from the clawing Drake defense, the Bruins could not get the ball to Alcindor. In fact, they were happy if they could get a pass off safely to anyone. With McCarter blazing away, Drake edged past UCLA twice in the second half. Alcindor practically disappeared from sight as he totaled only eight field goals for the game.

Unfortunately for Drake, their shooting was off during most of the game. But even with a poor 38.6% accuracy rate, they still came within a few points of upsetting UCLA. Only guard John Vallely's calm shooting (29 points) boosted UCLA to an 85-82 win. Drake's daring defensive challenge had turned an awkward mismatch into the most thrilling post-season game in Lew Alcindor's three-year reign as the ruler of college basketball.

Drake's Al Williams (41) and his teammate prevent Lew Alcindor from passing. Although the Bulldogs hounded Lew Alcindor tenaciously throughout the game, their effort to defeat the favored Bruins fell short.

2 Choose Your Desperation Shot

Cornbread Maxwell's 25-point performance against top-rated Michigan helped put UNC-Charlotte into the final four in 1977.

You are coaching the Marquette University Warriors.

With an unspectacular 23-7 mark, you are a little surprised to find yourself in the final four of the 1977 NCAA tournament. Yet you are the clear favorite over your opponent, an almost unknown team from the University of North Carolina at Charlotte.

The UNC-Charlotte 49'ers have made a tradition of knocking off favored teams ever since their shocking runner-up finish in the 1976 National Invitational Tournament. This year they are back to their old tricks as they beat the nation's number-one-ranked team, the University of Michigan, in their regional.

Now that there are only three seconds left in your semifinal match with UNC-Charlotte, you understand how they beat Michigan: they are very good and very lucky. After trailing 23-9 early in the game, UNC fought back to grab a 47-44 lead with less than two minutes remaining. Then it was your turn to scramble back on top as you took a 49-47 lead with less than 10 seconds to go. Despite a good defensive effort by your Warriors, the 49'ers' Cedric (Cornbread) Maxwell shoveled an awkward, off-balance shot toward the basket, and it dropped into the net to tie the score. Immediately, you called time out.

Three seconds remain in regulation time and the ball will be thrown in play under your defensive basket. How can you pull out a win and avoid a tense overtime against the tough 49'ers?

First consider your long-shot artists.

If there's anyone who can pull off a miraculous shot under this kind of pressure, it is probably your junior guard, Butch Lee. It was he who nearly turned the 1976 Olympics upside-down. Lee, a Puerto Rican who was raised in New York City, failed to make the United States' basketball squad that year and joined Puerto Rico's team instead. At the Olympics, he nearly pulled off the basketball upset of the century when he led his overmatched team to within one point of beating the eventual gold medalists from the United States, 95-94. Over the past season he has earned high marks for his clutch shooting.

Your other outside threat is Gary Rosenberger. Although Gary's play has not inspired enough confidence to win him a full-time starting job, the little guard is often called on to provide long-range scoring against zone defenses.

In the three seconds allowed, neither Gary nor Butch is likely to get off a shot from any closer than half court. While players have made such shots on rare occasions, the chances of it happening here are slim.

A determined Gary Rosenberger launches a long-range jumpshot for Marquette.

Inset: Butch Lee

21

Next, consider the possibility of a court-length pass.

You could have a player fire the ball all the way down to your offensive basket. One of your players might be able to come down with the "long pass" and get off a shot from close range. Possibly he may draw a foul and get a chance to win the game from the free-throw line.

This strategy would allow you to make use of the skills of senior Bo Ellis. After three years of setting up his teammates, this has been Bo's year to shine. The 6-foot, 9-inch, four-year starter is a cool, experienced forward. He can maneuver and shoot as well as rebound.

Along with Ellis, you count on the strength of 6-foot, 10-inch center Jerome Whitehead. Although

Muscular Jerome Whitehead strains for a Marquette rebound.

he is still learning to get the most out of his bruising physique, Whitehead is improving with every game. He joins Ellis in giving you a power advantage over the 49'ers. Opposing these two, however, is Cedric Maxwell, who has pulled off some fine plays under pressure.

Another matter of concern is the scoreboard. In this Atlanta arena, it is suspended over the center of the court. A good pass will avoid hitting the scoreboard, but if the pass should strike it, that could mean disaster. The ball would then go to UNC-Charlotte under your defensive basket, giving them an excellent chance to win.

What's Your Decision?

You are the coach.
Remember that the clock will not start until the ball is touched inbounds by a player.
What do you call for in your sideline huddle?

#1 Have Lee throw a fullcourt pass up for grabs near the basket.

#2 Have Ellis pass in to Lee who takes the desperation shot.

#3 Have Ellis pass into Rosenberger who takes the desperation shot.

#4 Have Whitehead lob to Ellis at center court, and Ellis relay to Lee for a 35-foot shot.

Choose the play. Then turn the page to find out which play the Marquette coach chose.

Marquette looked to choice #1 for the winning points.

After walking on the court to inspect the position of the scoreboard, Marquette coach Al McGuire chose Lee to throw in the pass. He counted on his star guard to have the sense to avoid hitting it with a wild pass. With two top rebounders in Ellis and Whitehead, the Warriors figured to have a slight advantage over the smaller 49'ers in coming down with the long pass. The odds against a shot going in from beyond center court seemed to be too great (#2 and #3). And UNC-Charlotte's defense, which had held the Warriors to only 49 points, was probably too good to allow Marquette to complete two passes and a shot within three seconds (#4).

Here's What Happened!

Lee stepped back and fired a baseball pass that avoided the scoreboard and came down near the free-throw line in Marquette's offensive court. Ellis had slightly better position than his UNC-Charlotte opponents, and he went up high after the ball. But Lee's throw was too strong and it bounced off Ellis' fingertips. UNC's Maxwell, jumping at the same time, then had a chance to grab it. But the deflection off Ellis caused the ball to sail through Cedric's hands and into the waiting arms of Whitehead! It took an agonizingly long time for Whitehead to turn and attempt the lay-up. But as a desperate Maxwell flew by in his bid to block the shot, the ball struck the rim and finally bounced in.

The clock, however, had shown that time had run out about the time the ball left Whitehead's hands. For a few seconds, the court was overrun with chaos as the referee met with the official timekeeper. Finally, they declared that the shot had been made within the time allowed. Marquette had pulled off an almost impossible play to beat the 49'ers, 51-49, and they went on to beat the University of North Carolina for the 1977 NCAA title.

3 The Unstoppable Elgin Baylor

How can the Wildcats come between Baylor and the basket?

You are coaching the University of Kentucky Wildcats.

The NCAA finals are nothing new for you, since your school has been the most successful in NCAA history. You've already won three national titles and would like to add this 1958 trophy to your collection. But no Kentucky team has ever had to face anything quite like Elgin Baylor. The 23-year-old star of the Seattle University Chieftains seems to be years ahead of his rivals.

Because of the soft schedule they played, many have their doubts about the Seattle team. Yet it is obvious that any team that starts the 6-foot, 5-inch Baylor will present its opponent with problems. And the truth is that this is not one of your best Kentucky teams. Their 22-6 mark during the season got them no better than a number-14 ranking among major college teams.

You are aware that you don't have a player who is even close to Baylor in ability. You've seen other coaches try a variety of tricks to shut out Elgin, but he has always made his share of points and defensive plays. How do you plan a strategy against someone who seems impossible to stop?

Baylor's statistics are frightening.

The star from Washington, D.C., rebounds like a center, is quicker than most guards, and jumps like a kangaroo. With his midair body balance, he gets off good shots against the tightest defenses. Baylor has so many moves that he could probably run through a briar patch without getting scratched. His 31.3 career scoring average ranks second in NCAA history, and he has also pulled down more than 20 rebounds per game. Baylor showed how explosive he can be in a game against Portland when he scored 60 points.

Check out Baylor's teammates for fresh clues as to how to play Seattle.

The Chieftains have won 19 of their last 20 games mainly on their deadly shooting. Baylor is not the only long-range artist on the team. Charlie Brown, Jerry Frizzell, and Don Ogorek also get their share of points. It's tough to plan against Seattle because they are not a predictable team. They like to try freelance moves and make split-second, on-the-run decisions.

Their main weaknesses are size and defense. The 6-foot, 5-inch Baylor, although a natural forward, plays center for the Chieftains. He is the team's best inside defender and its only consistent rebounder. On a team hurting for defensive skills, Baylor may be just as valuable to Seattle for his defensive work.

Here the Chieftains display their teamwork, with 6'3" Charlie Brown shooting from the inside and Elgin Baylor positioning himself for a rebound.

29

Look at the strengths of your own team.

Your Wildcats do everything just opposite from the way Seattle does things. You don't have any stars or anyone capable of firing from 20 feet. Instead, your team patiently works the ball around until a good shot opens up. They are excellent passers who run disciplined patterns and play heads-up defense.

Kentucky's John Cox, shown here going for a lay-up, can also be counted on for long-distance shooting.

Much of the offense comes from inside drives off of set plays. Vernon Hatton, John Crigler, and John Cox can leave defenses dizzy as they weave in and out of the middle. Center Ed Beck contributes some reliable defensive work but is not an aggressive scorer or rebounder. He is going to need help in stopping Baylor. With four seniors and one junior in the starting lineup, you have an experienced unit that has learned to play together as a team.

What's Your Decision?

You are the coach.
If Baylor plays his usual all-around game, it's going to be tough for your team to win.
How will you stop Baylor?

#1 Keep the ball away from Baylor on offense and defense.

#2 Try to get Baylor in foul trouble by directing your play <u>at</u> him.

#3 Double-team and triple-team Baylor on defense.

Choose the strategy. Then turn the page to find out which strategy the Kentucky coach chose.

Kentucky chose #2.

Baylor had so much more skill than other college players that he could probably dominate the game unless he ran into foul trouble. The Wildcats chose to attack Baylor with their offensive plays. They had plenty of players who could drive into the lane and draw fouls in such close quarters. Baylor might be especially hurt by such a plan because he could not expect much help from his teammates on defense. Even if Elgin avoided fouling, he would have to work so hard on defense that he would have little energy left for offense.

Unlike many big men who dominate, Baylor is quick and handles the ball well. That makes it harder to seal him off from the ball (#1). Seattle's other fine outside shooters make it risky to rely on double-teaming to win the game (#3).

Here's What Happened!

Kentucky went into a complicated offense with quick passes and constant switching of positions. During these dizzying maneuvers, the Seattle defenders were forced to change their defensive assignments. The Wildcat strategy forced Baylor to switch over to guarding the quick-driving John Crigler. Elgin's hustling attempts to catch and stop Crigler's drives resulted in fouls. Baylor was saddled with three fouls before the game was 10 minutes old.

Although Kentucky's strategy seemed to be working against Baylor, Seattle did not let it bother them. Baylor gamely played on, a little more cautiously, and Seattle still led 39-36 at halftime. With their star center working furiously at both ends of the court, the Chieftains moved out to a 44-38 lead at the start of the second half. Then, with just over 16 minutes remaining, Baylor was charged with his fourth foul.

Seattle had to do something to protect Elgin on defense so he would not foul out of the game. They moved him under the basket and lined up the rest of the team in a zone to keep the ball out of the middle. Wildcats Hatton and Cox then shot the zone to pieces and the Kentucky crew started to roll. Pulling ahead for the first time at 61-60, they kept going until they had gained a comfortable 84-72 win. Free from the threat of the aggressive Baylor, Hatton pumped in 30 points and Cox had 24.

Even with his burden of fouls, Baylor still contributed 25 points and 19 rebounds. Observers agreed that if Baylor had stayed clear of fouls throughout the game, the result probably would have been different. Credit an aggressive offensive plan with helping Kentucky to their fourth national title.

Kentucky gets the upper hand as Wildcat center Ed Beck (34) blocks an Elgin Baylor shot. Looking on are Seattle's Don Ogorek (53) and Kentucky forward John Crigler (32).

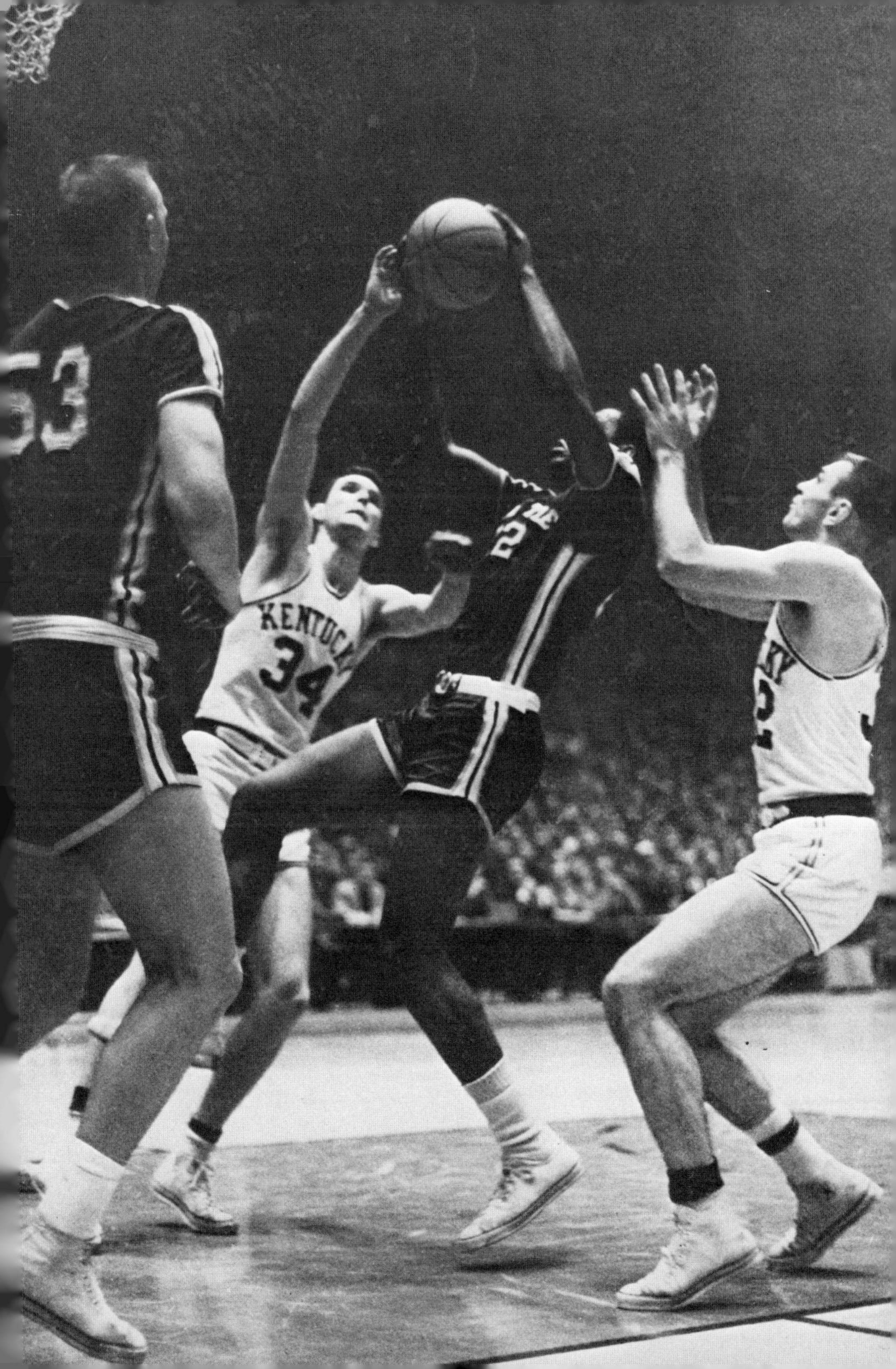
KENTUCKY
34

4 The Dangers of Playing It Safe

Tim Stoddard (42), shown here in season play, missed the game-winning shot in the last seconds of your semifinal contest with UCLA. Now in overtime, you have another chance to win—or lose.

You are coaching the North Carolina State University Wolfpack.

Although this is only a semifinal match, almost everyone believes that this game will determine the winner of the 1974 NCAA title. College basketball fans, tired of UCLA's monotonous winning streak, have been waiting two years for this showdown. North Carolina State went undefeated in 1973 and appeared to be the one team strong enough to challenge the Bruins. But because of recruiting violations, the Wolfpack was banned from the NCAA tournament, and UCLA claimed its seventh straight championship. This year, NC State has been allowed back in the tourney and is ranked number two behind UCLA.

So far the game has been everything anyone could ask for. UCLA forged a 57-46 lead in the second half, but the Wolfpack reeled off 10 straight points to get back in the game. Your team had a chance to win the game in regulation time as you played for one last shot. But forward Tim Stoddard missed an open shot from the corner. Now the game, tied at 65-65, has moved into overtime and you have the ball. It's tempting to play it safe and protect the ball so that you get the only shot of the overtime. Will you?

Look at the players you face in battling the Bruins.

This is the dreaded "Walton Gang," a team that has proven to be even greater than Lew Alcindor's powerhouse Bruins. Led by 6-foot, 11-inch center Bill Walton, UCLA smashed the University of San Francisco's record 60-game winning streak by reeling off 88 straight wins! Walton may not be the consistent scoring machine that Alcindor was, but he gets his share of baskets. In last year's title game against Memphis State, he broke a championship game record by scoring 44 points while missing only one shot! Already he is probably a better passer and defender than any center in the pros. As a yardstick of his brilliance, he is a strong favorite to win his third straight award as the United Press International's College Player of the Year.

Walton's supporting cast is loaded with stars. Keith "Silk" Wilkes joins Walton as a first-team All-American. The 6-foot, 6-inch forward is a strong all-around player and certain first-round pro draft choice. The other forward is Dave Meyers who, in contrast to the graceful Wilkes, plays like a cornered wildcat. He is a rugged defender and rebounder who also has the skill to start in the pros.

The backcourt is not as spectacular. Tommy Curtis and Greg Lee provide steady play at the guard spots, but they don't always dominate their opponents. They lead UCLA's famous fullcourt press. UCLA's latest win, an 83-60 win over a strong University of San Francisco team, shows that they are again peaking for the championship.

All-Americans Keith Wilkes (left) and Bill Walton lead UCLA's incomparable Walton Gang.

Your own team sports an unusual collection of stars in three sizes.

Your medium-size star, David Thompson, shines the brightest. The 6-foot, 4-inch forward bounds high above the rim as though the entire court were a trampoline. He has caught up to several passes thrown high above the basket and dunked them for points. With his accurate and unblockable jump shots, he has come on late in the game to give Keith Wilkes fits.

North Carolina State's giant-size star is center Tommy Burleson who, at a gangly 7 feet, 4 inches, actually dwarfs Walton. Although not nearly the natural athlete nor all-around performer that Walton is, Burleson has given UCLA's red-haired star a tough game. His clutch baskets over Walton have helped to keep the game close.

David Thompson

Tommy Burleson

Standing nearly two feet lower to the floor is guard Monte Towe. The 5-foot, 5-inch guard looks like a midget scooting around among the other players. But not only has he survived as a college basketball starter, he has become one of your most important players. Flitting in and out of the defenses while opposing guards struggle to keep up, Towe directs the Wolfpack offense and has done well at dribbling through the UCLA press.

Pint-sized Monte Towe is an expert at finding cracks in the defense.

Your cautious nature tells you that it might be best to play for one shot.

You aren't sure that your players are quite as good as the Bruins. UCLA's long record of success, their deep roster full of high school All-Americans, and their easy, 18-point victory over you back in December point to that conclusion. It might be best, therefore, not to get into a shooting contest with them. Basketball experts say that a slowdown game is usually to the advantage of the underdog.

Ordinarily it might be foolish to try and play keep-away for five minutes from the Bruins' tough defensive press, but Towe has done well at avoiding turnovers so far. If you can hang onto the ball until 10 seconds remain, then you can start a play and get a chance for a good shot, leaving UCLA with no time to retaliate.

But you also know that too much caution can lose a game.

You already tried this strategy during the last minute of regulation time and didn't win with it. There are two dangers in trying it again. First, the pressure of a championship overtime can be unbearable. It's asking a lot of your players to throw the ball around for five minutes without making a single mistake. If you do turn the ball over, you will have wasted an important scoring chance.

Secondly, this timid strategy may indicate that you are afraid to challenge UCLA and are trying to squeak out a championship on luck. Should the strategy fail, you run the risk that your team will lose its confidence and alertness. Since the game is being played in your home state at Greensboro, North Carolina, you also run the risk of turning the Wolfpack fans against you with your unpopular stalling tactics.

What's Your Decision?

You are the coach.
Monte Towe is bouncing the ball, looking for a signal from you.
What will you tell him to do?

#1 Slow down the game and play for one shot.

#2 Start working immediately for a shot.

Choose your play. Then turn the page to find out which play the North Carolina State coach chose.

North Carolina State selected #1.

As the underdog in the game, they went with the underdog's strategy. Gambling that Monte Towe could continue to keep control of the ball, they wanted to make sure that UCLA had no chance to get even one shot in the overtime period.

Here's What Happened!

The Wolfpack held on to the ball, pretending that the basket did not exist. The minutes ticked by as the fans, growing hoarse and nearly as exhausted as the players, watched the maddening stall. Towe managed to keep the ball away from the Bruins, and with 10 seconds left in the overtime, the Wolfpack finally went into action. Thompson drove into the lane, jumped high, and twisted away from his opponents. But the Walton Gang was right there with him and Thompson quickly passed off to Burleson. Tall Tommy was open for a second, but his shot bounced off the rim and the overtime period ended. NC State had blown another chance, and the game remained tied.

Teams rarely got a third chance against UCLA. The Bruins quickly took charge in the second overtime period, and they surged into a commanding five-point lead. While the Bruins played aggressively, at first the Wolfpack seemed trapped by the slow pace they had set in the previous overtime.

Jolted into action by their desperate situation, the Wolfpack responded with brilliant shooting and game-saving defense. It was the veteran Bruins who made the mistakes as North Carolina State roared from behind to win the game, 80-77. UCLA's long reign as champ had finally ended, but only after North Carolina was forced out of its own one-shot strategy.

Tommy Burleson's 20 points and 14 rebounds helped North Carolina State upset UCLA. Here he shoots over superstar Bill Walton, who could not contain him.

5 Workhorses vs. Greyhounds

Willie Worsley (upper left), Orsten Artis (right), and Bobby Joe Hill are three of the workhorses Texas Western depended on to gain a spot in this 1966 title contest.

You are coaching the Texas Western College Miners.

The NCAA finals are a new experience for your El Paso school, which has never been this close to a title in any sport. But even though none of your players are All-American candidates, you have shown that you belong in the finals. Tough defense, fierce rebounding, and fine teamwork have powered you to a 26-1 record and a number-three national ranking.

The big test comes next, however, when you meet the top-ranked University of Kentucky. Not only are the Wildcats considered the best in the country, they also have the kind of quick, small team that has given you trouble all year. How do you prepare for this 1966 title game?

The Wildcats are unbelievably small but vastly talented.

Kentucky coach Adolph Rupp doesn't have a starting player taller than 6 feet, 5 inches. Both 6-foot, 5-inch center Thad Jaracz and thin 6-foot, 3-inch forward Larry Conley seemed hopelessly overmatched at their positions. But "Rupp's Runts," as they are called, make up for this with deadly shooting and an attacking defense. Conley is really a guard masquerading as a forward. His quick hands and intelligent passes help him direct the offense from the forward spot while the guards take over the scoring load.

Wildcat guards Louis Dampier and Pat Riley are dangerous shots from any range. When they are hot, the Wildcats don't have to depend on wrestling away offensive rebounds from taller opponents. Dampier, an All-American, led Kentucky's attack in the semifinal against Duke with 23 points, while Riley added 19.

Kentucky's speed and teamwork have made it tough for opponents to overpower them. When playing against large, rugged teams, the Wildcats usually fall back into a 1-3-1 zone defense. This defense chokes off movement near the basket and dares opponents to shoot from long range. The 1-3-1 enabled Kentucky to beat Dayton earlier in the tournament despite the Flyers' strong 6-foot, 11-inch center, Henry Finkel.

Though small in stature, Kentucky's Wildcats, including Tommy Kron (30), Larry Conley (40), and Pat Riley (42), are big in basketball skill.

Your team doesn't play well against Kentucky's brand of defense.

The best way to beat a tight zone is to hit on outside shots. That forces defenders to come out from under the basket to guard you more closely. But outside shooting isn't a strong point with your group. Among your starters, only 6-foot, 1-inch guard Orsten Artis makes any attempt at outside shooting. The other guard, 5-foot, 9-inch Bobby Joe Hill, is a cobra-quick defender and driver, but he's not likely to find much driving room against the 1-3-1. Reserve guard Willie Worsley combines quickness and a shooting touch, as shown by his 12 points in the semifinal against Utah. But Worsley is only 5 feet, 6 inches tall, and he can't defend like Hill or score like Artis.

Willie Worsley

Orsten Artis

You could add quickness to your attack with a three-guard offense. Most teams that try that, though, have at least one fairly large guard; yours range from small to tiny.

Bobby Joe Hill

You have more than enough muscle at the forward spots. Your Miners led the entire nation in rebounding percentage this season. The largest and fiercest of your players is 6-foot, 7-inch, 240-pound David Lattin. Opponents think twice before challenging this immovable object in the middle.

Nevil Shed and Harry Flournoy are also at their best when crashing the backboards for rebounds. As if they needed any help, forward Willie Cager can do much the same thing when he comes off the bench. None of these musclemen is particularly quick, however, and none likes to stray too far from the basket.

What's Your Decision?

You are the coach.
There's no doubt in your mind that Kentucky will start out in a tight 1-3-1 defense.
What will you do to combat it?

#1 Go to the three-guard lineup, taking out one of your forwards.

#2 Substitute Worsley for Hill.

#3 Slow down play until Kentucky grows impatient and comes out of their defensive shell.

#4 Play a running game. Grab rebounds and fire passes the length of the court for easy lay-ups.

Choose the offense. Then turn the page to find out which offense the Texas Western coach chose.

Texas Western went with choice #1.

The Miners had such confidence in the overwhelming strength of Lattin and the other forward that they felt they could afford to go with a very small lineup. They hoped their rebounding edge was so great that they could still beat Kentucky on the boards with only two big men. Kentucky's lack of size made it possible for the Miners to use three guards even though Texas Western's guards were unusually small. That would give them the quickness and outside shooting to work against the Wildcats' zone defense.

There would be no point in substituting Worsley for Hill (#2) as you would just be replacing one valuable, quick player with another quick player. Texas Western's attempts to slow down the game may not have any effect (#3) on a disciplined Kentucky team. The Wildcats' overall edge in quickness would make it difficult to beat them with only fastbreak baskets (#4).

Here's What Happened!

Little Willie Worsley took over the starting spot of Nevil Shed, who stood a foot taller. Still, the menacing "Big Daddy" Lattin and Harry Flournoy were able to keep the Miners' edge near the basket.

With the score tied at 9-9, the Miners' trio of slick guards went to work. Bobby Joe Hill darted in to steal the ball from Tommy Kron and zoomed the length of the court for a lay-up. While the Wildcats were still kicking themselves for that mistake, Hill stole another pass and again scored, giving the Miners a 13-9 lead.

Kentucky's efforts to catch up were slowed by the Texas Western defense. Dampier and Riley rarely found any openings in the defense and had to sink difficult shots just to stay close. In the second half, the Wildcats closed to within one point, but Artis and Hill led another spurt that put the Miners ahead to stay.

Texas Western's strategy worked to perfection. The three guards combined for 43 points while Lattin's intimidating presence held each of Kentucky's front line players to 10 points or less. The Miners won the game, 72-65.

Bobby Joe Hill's sensational steal from Tommy Kron was the first of two steals that broke the game open for the Miners.

6 Off to Beat the Wizard

A shouting John Wooden displays the aggressive style of coaching that has led UCLA to nine NCAA titles in 11 years. Can you stop him before he gets a tenth title?

You are coaching the University of Louisville Cardinals.

This is no time to be sentimental. It may be UCLA coach John Wooden's last tournament before retiring at the end of a great career, but you would like to see him go out a loser.

In this 1975 semifinal contest, you've had several opportunities to end the magic of the "Wizard of Westwood," as Wooden is known. With only 1:06 left in the game, your team held a 65-61 lead. But UCLA's fullcourt press came to life and forced you to make key mistakes. As a result, the game went into overtime.

Now you have another chance. You are ahead 74-73 with less than a minute remaining, and your team has control of the ball. You can't afford to let this lead slip away. What will you do?

There are enough good players at your school to stock two winning teams.

Your Cardinals had won 27 of 29 games going into this contest. You have five capable starters and waves of reserves who are nearly as good. In fact, some of the reserves have been starters for you in past seasons.

Forwards Wesley Cox and Junior Bridgeman usually lead your offense, but they've been quiet for most of the game. Cox has been slowed by a leg injury and has contributed just 14 points so far. Bridgeman has been caught up in a ferocious duel with his high school teammate, Pete Trgovich. Trgovich held Bridgeman to 12 points but fouled out in the process.

As a result, most of your team's scoring has been done by guard Allen Murphy. The Bruins weren't prepared for him and have stared helplessly as he has drilled home 33 points. None of your other players has scored as many as 10 points.

The UCLA press really should not pose that much of a problem to you. Since you have more good reserves than the Bruins have, you have been able to rest your players more during the game. They should be fresh enough and quick enough to keep a step ahead of the pursuing Bruins. Yet how do you explain the collapse at the end of the game?

Wesley Cox

Allen Murphy

It may be that a free throw will decide the game.

If you chose to kill time by passing the ball around, UCLA is likely to foul intentionally to get the ball back. In that case, you want to make sure that a good shooter is fouled.

You have two good ballhandlers who also shoot free throws well. The first is Murphy, who has connected on five of seven free throws in this game. He also seems to have the hot hand at the moment and has scored seven of your team's nine overtime points.

Terry Howard, a reserve, is the second man who seems ideal for this situation. A starter in past years, Howard is an excellent dribbler with an incredible free-throw record. This season he has made <u>all</u> of his free-throw tries! The only thing that might make you hesitate to use him is the fact that he would be coming in cold. Terry hasn't played much tonight and hasn't tried a shot in the game.

Junior Bridgeman, your 6-foot, 5-inch forward, is also a top free-throw shooter, the best among your starters. He has held up well to the pressure of championship ball by sinking all four of his free shots in this game. Bridgeman also has the quickness and passing skills to switch over to a guard position.

The best way to insure that one of these men is fouled is to play a "four corners" offense. In this setup, you place an offensive player in each of the four corners of the offensive court. This spreads out the defense and gives your fifth man plenty of room to dribble around and make a pass if he has to. Since this fifth man controls the ball most of the time, there is a good chance it is he who will draw the foul.

Terry Howard, shown here during the season, has a flawless free-throw record this year.

Take a look at the Bruin defense.

For the first time in years, UCLA does not have a dominating center. Seven-foot, one-inch Ralph Drollinger has not been able to fill Bill Walton's shoes. John Wooden's team also lacks its usual huge advantage in play-off experience.

Marques Johnson's poise and ability on the court is tempered by his lack of play-off experience.

Other than 6-foot, 7-inch senior forward David Meyers, the Bruin stars are inexperienced sophomores. Richard Washington, a surprisingly quick, 6-foot, 10-inch forward, and super-athlete Marques Johnson own great all-around ability, but they haven't gone through this kind of pressure before.

The UCLA press, led by guard Andre McCarter, can't be overlooked, however. They already forced one key turnover. Perhaps there is something about the great Coach Wooden that gets exceptional performances out of players at crucial times.

What's Your Decision?

You are the coach.
With less than a minute left in the game, the Wizard is giving final instructions to his players.
What instructions will you give to your team?

#1 Spread out into a "four corners" offense with Murphy doing most of the ball-handling.

#2 Use the "four corners," and bring in Howard to run it.

#3 Let Murphy drive for a shot.

#4 Keep the ball moving between Murphy, Howard, and Bridgeman.

Choose the play. Then turn the page to find out which play the Louisville coach chose.

Louisville selected choice #2.

Although it was a tough spot for someone who wasn't fully warmed up, Louisville could not resist that 100% free-throw record. Since Terry Howard was a fine dribbler as well as shooter, the ball seemed safest left in his hands. When UCLA resorted to the desperation foul, Howard was a good bet to make the two free throws that would put the game out of reach.

Choice #3 was eliminated simply because of the risk. When you take a shot, you give up control of the ball, and once you do that, you've given the other team a chance to win.

Murphy and Bridgeman would also have been good choices to shoot free throws, but Louisville trusted Howard to "do his thing."

Here's What Happened!

Howard grabbed the ball and Louisville's four other players spread out toward the edges of the court. UCLA then had to cover the entire court, which made it difficult for their press to trap Terry or his teammates. The Bruins could not force a Cardinal error and finally had to foul Howard with 20 seconds left in the game.

Howard stepped to the free-throw line facing a one-and-one situation: if he made the first free throw, he would be rewarded with an extra free-throw attempt. But as the Cardinal fans watched in horror, Howard's shot bounced off the rim, his first miss of the year.

UCLA called for a time out with 13 seconds to go. Coach Wooden set up a play for his tall forward, Washington, who worked his way into the middle and put up a soft 10-foot shot. The ball dropped through the net, giving the Bruins a 75-74 overtime win. Louisville's overtime strategy had been working to perfection but fell short for one frustrating reason: in sports, there is no such thing as a sure thing.

The Bruins' win over Louisville put them in the 1975 title contest against Kentucky. Here John Wooden walks off the court after his final victory—a 92-85 triumph over Kentucky in the NCAA championship game.

7 Taking the Gola Challenge

Tom Gola, three-time All-American and 1954 MVP,
moves in for the rebound.
Can the San Francisco Dons move him out?

You are coaching the University of San Francisco Dons.

Few coaches can boast of having built such a solid basketball program in as short a time as you have. Your Dons have been so impressive during this 1954-55 college season that they have risen from being unranked to becoming the number-one rated team in the NCAA. Not bad for a team that posted a 45-49 record over the past four years and does not even have a gymnasium large enough to host any home games!

In the finals of this 1955 NCAA tournament, however, you must risk your ranking and your 27-1 record against the defending champions, the LaSalle Explorers. This college team from Philadelphia, 26-4 this season, relies heavily on 6-foot, 6-inch center Tom Gola to power their offense.

You have a fine center of your own, Bill Russell. This 6-foot, 10-inch athlete has developed into a defensive wonder in his junior year. Do you want to challenge Gola to a head-to-head contest with Russell, or will you turn to a different strategy to shut off the LaSalle star?

In his four years as a starter, Gola has trampled most of his opponents.

Even as a freshman, this home-grown Philadelphia star powered the Explorers to a championship. It was Gola's fine play that helped LaSalle win the National Invitational Tournament in 1952. In the three years since then, reporters have run out of compliments for him. Tom has scored as many as 54 points in a single game and has been named an All-American for three years. He holds the NCAA record for most rebounds in a career with 2,201.

Along with his height and strength, Tom is blessed with great reflexes and a smooth shooting touch. He shows the all-around coordination you would expect from an athlete who was a four-event track star. But perhaps his most outstanding trait is the way he responds to pressure. His coolness led LaSalle to the NCAA title the year before.

Judging by his 23 points in the semifinal against Iowa, Gola is as ready as ever to go for a championship. Although LaSalle expects scoring from other players such as Charley Singley (who scored 16 against Iowa), you know that shutting down Gola is the key to beating LaSalle.

As the nation's top defensive college team, you have some weapons that may work against Gola.

The key man in your defense is your surprising young center, Bill Russell. As a poor shooting, 6-foot, 6-inch senior at McClymonds High School in Oakland, California, Russell failed to impress any recruiters. But after enrolling at San Francisco, his hidden talents burst into the open. Now standing 6 feet, 10 inches tall, Bill has shown that a center can dominate a game even if he isn't a great shooter. Russell is a cagey defender with great leaping skill and mousetrap reflexes. Players who venture into the lane against the Dons usually find their lay-up tries stuffed back in their faces. That unsettling experience often causes players to alter their shots so that they can arch them over Russell's outstretched hands. Despite his aggressive defense, Russell rarely draws fouls. He is an excellent rebounder and has learned how to score well enough to chip in about 20 points per game. Your main concern about him may be his lack of big-game experience.

Bill Russell's specialty is defense, but when he is close to the basket he can also score.

Russell is not the only defensive star on your team, though. Many who saw your 62-50 semifinal win over Colorado marveled at the play of guard K.C. Jones. Jones was another unrecruited high school athlete who wound up playing great defense for San Francisco. Only 6 feet, 1 inch tall, Jones soared high enough to pull rebounds away from much taller Colorado players.

The expert advice of Russell and Jones has helped your entire team play well on defense. Guard Hal Perry, forwards Stan Buchanan and Jerry Mullen, and a host of reserves all helped the Dons lead the NCAA by allowing only 52.1 points per game. The Dons are not shy about calling on reserve strength, either. Twelve players saw action in the Colorado contest.

What's Your Decision?

You are the coach.
Your team is waiting to hear how they can stop the famous Tom Gola.
What's your strategy?

#1 Match Russell against Gola.

#2 Use your bench strength to shuffle in fresh players to guard Gola in hopes of tiring him out.

#3 Give K.C. Jones the task of guarding Gola and leave Russell under the basket as a last line of defense.

Choose your strategy. Then turn the page to find out which strategy the San Francisco coach chose.

San Francisco chose #3.

Although Jones was giving away five inches in height and was a guard rather than a center, the Dons gave him the job of stopping Gola. In the words of the stunned Jones, the move "blew my whole dinner." But his coach felt that Jones' extraordinary spring could help make up for his height disadvantage. Also, the experience of playing against a small, quick guard might be one of the few things that Tom hadn't seen before on a basketball court.

Choice #1 was turned down because of the fear that Gola might try to draw Russell away from the basket and open up the middle of the Dons' defense. With Jones taking care of Gola, Russell could stay in the lane to frighten off all comers with his menacing arms. Also, Russell would be free to dominate the rebounding.

A superb athlete such as Gola was not likely to be worn out by a defense made up of lesser San Francisco players (#2).

Here's What Happened!

Freed from the burden of watching Gola, Russell terrorized the Explorers around the basket. While keeping LaSalle from shooting at close range, he scored 18 points in the first half, mainly on tap-ins. Rebounds were his exclusive property, as he totaled 25 for the game.

Gola, meanwhile, had a terrible time prying himself loose from the pesky Jones. Although Jones called Gola the toughest player he ever guarded in college ball, K.C. was equal to the challenge. Gola could never get loose in the game, and with his shooting form thrown off stride, he tallied only 16 points. Jones not only held the Explorer star well below his usual totals, he also outscored him. With 18 second-half points, K.C. finished the game with 24 points, one more than his teammate Russell. San Francisco's clever strategy helped produce a surprisingly easy 77-63 win.

San Francisco forward Stan Buchanan (15) plays tight defense against LaSalle's Alonzo Lewis (5), while Bill Russell stations himself in familiar territory—under the basket.

8 Senior Honors

Jack Givens

Rick Robey

Mike Phillips

You are coaching the University of Kentucky Wildcats.

What do you get when you put an extremely talented group of young basketball players together at a school with a tremendous basketball program and tradition? Misery! At least that has been the unfortunate fate of the seniors on your 1978 team. They have played brilliantly for the past four years but have received little credit. For one reason, your team made the finals of the 1975 NCAA tournament when many of these players were only freshmen. Kentucky fans assumed that they could look forward to at least a couple of championships in the years to come as their NCAA runner-up team improved. But the Wildcats have not even made it to the final four the past two seasons.

This year has been the last chance for these seniors, and the pressure on them has been enormous. So far they have gritted their teeth and survived. After a narrow win over Michigan State in the regionals, they held off Arkansas to advance to the championship against the Duke Blue Devils.

Right now you have a 13-point lead over Duke with less than two minutes left to play. Your seniors have outplayed Duke all the way and are on the verge of finally winning that NCAA title. It is an emotional time for your team. You would like to show your appreciation by letting your seniors finish their careers in style. It would be a fitting honor to pull the starters out of the game while time still remained so that they could accept the hard-earned applause of the crowd. Thirteen points seems a comfortable cushion with so little time left. When is the best time to take out your seniors?

Consider your senior-dominated team.

Forward Jack "Goose" Givens has been simply awesome in this contest. Duke foolishly left a gap in their defense near the foul line and Givens made them pay for the mistake. With his teammates feeding passes to him in that area, Givens poured in Kentucky's last 16 points of the first half to give them a 45-38 lead. He has continued to hit that shot, connecting on 18 of 27 shots so far in the game. His total of 41 points is within reach of Bill Walton's championship record of 44.

Besides Givens, you have twin towers Rick Robey and Mike Phillips. Both stand 6 feet, 10 inches, and help you dominate play near the basket. In this game, Robey has contributed 20 points. Another key senior is James Lee, a bruising 6-foot, 5-inch, 240-pound forward who provides a lift when he comes off the bench.

No one has been able to stop Jack Givens in this game. Here he shoots over Duke defender Jim Spanarkel for two of his 41 championship game points.

Check out your opponents, the Duke Blue Devils.

Duke is a very young team, much like your Wildcats of three years ago. They were not impressive early in the year but have come on to post a 27-6 record. With impressive tournament victories over Villanova and Notre Dame, they have been playing near their peak. As a surprising entry in the final four, with no seniors in their lineup, Duke probably does not feel the awesome pressure that your team does.

The score seems to indicate that you have Duke outmanned in this game, but that may not be entirely true. Their strategy and their defensive work have put them into a big hole. Actually, three of their players are being watched closely by the

Mike Gminski

pros. Sophomore Mike Gminski, a 6-foot, 11-inch center, gives Duke strength up the middle. Even with the rugged tandem of Robey and Phillips leaning on him, Gminski has scored over 20 points.

Freshman Gene Banks is a 6-foot, 7-inch combination of muscles and moves. He can rebound, run, and score from the inside or outside. Duke also likes to run the ball and, as a team, has more speed than most give them credit for. Junior guard Jim Spanarkel, a 6-foot, 5-inch floor leader, is especially good at triggering a fast break.

What's Your Decision?

You are the coach.
You want to recognize your players, but you don't want to put the game in danger. You have a 13-point lead with two minutes to go. **What will you do?**

#1 Wait until 10 seconds remain, call time out and take out all the seniors at once.
#2 Keep the starters in, and feed Givens so that he can break Walton's record.
#3 Play the starters all the way.
#4 Start taking starters out now so that each can get an individual round of applause.

Choose the strategy. Then turn the page to find out which strategy the Kentucky coach chose.

Kentucky decided on #4.

A 13-point lead with so little time left seemed safe. The Wildcats wanted to recognize each individual senior, and in order to make sure that each had his moment, they would have to start now.

Here's What Happened!

The Kentucky starters began to leave the game, one at a time, to the wild cheers of their supporters. But the grins and back-slapping started to fade as the Blue Devils quickly whittled away at the lead. The Wildcat reserves could not seem to keep the ball out of Duke's hands. The discomfort turned to something near panic as the lead fell to six points with 23 seconds left.

Kentucky sheepishly hustled the starters back into the game to stop the furious Duke rally. For a moment it seemed as if it were too late to turn the tide. Duke made another basket to slice the margin to four points. Finally, James Lee broke loose from the gambling Duke defense and stuffed the ball to clinch the 94-88 win.

Wildcat backers breathed a sigh of relief as they mulled over the results of Kentucky's senior tribute. It came dangerously close to costing them the game. Basketball fans discovered the truth of the words attributed to baseball great Yogi Berra: "The game ain't over until it's over!"

After his team's near disaster, Kentucky's Most Valuable Player Jack Givens calmly clips the netting as a championship souvenir.

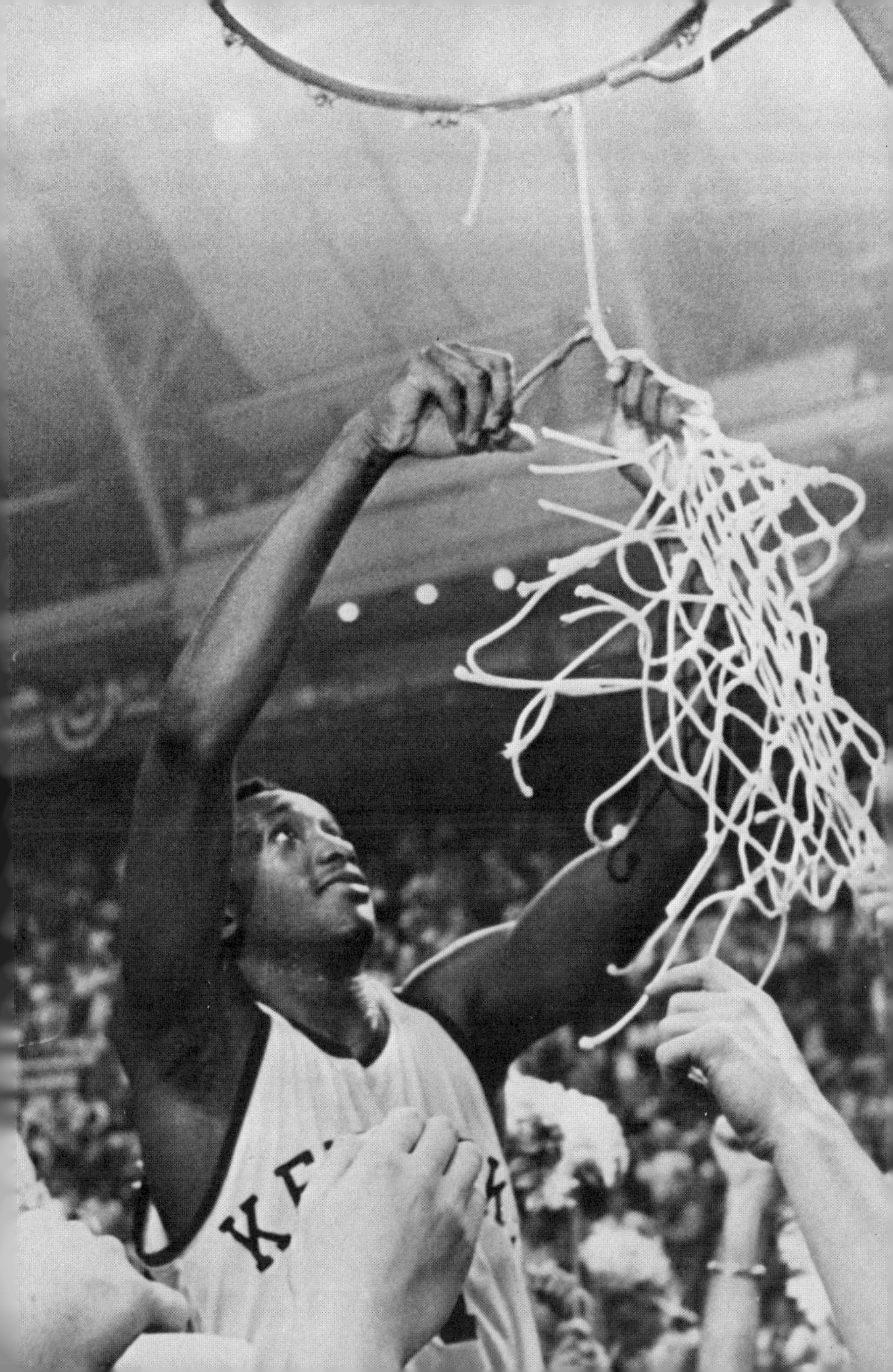

9 Axing Carolina's Tall Timber

The Indiana Hoosiers must find a way to trim North Carolina's tall trio of Sam Perkins (upper left), James Worthy (right), and Al Wood.

You are coaching the Indiana University Hoosiers.

There are three tall reasons why you find your team trailing the University of North Carolina in the 1981 NCAA final. The Tar Heels' lean and lanky front line of Al Wood, James Worthy, and Sam Perkins has been taking over the space above the basket. With 9:23 left in the first half, your Hoosiers trail, 16-8.

Yours is not an explosive team. In fact, as your 25-9 record shows, you may not have the talent that most championship finalists have. You cannot afford to get too far behind. This is especially true since North Carolina is the master of the lead-protecting "four corners" offense. Your current front line seems to be poorly matched against the leapers from North Carolina. Can you make some adjustments to get back into the game?

North Carolina probably has the finest front line in college basketball.

In tournament play, their threesome has done well at backing up that claim. All have size, speed, quickness, moves, and good hands.

The main weapon is 6-foot, 6-inch senior forward Al Wood. The Tar Heels' leading scorer, with a 17.5 average, has been on a campaign lately to convince pro scouts of his worth. In the early rounds of the NCAA tourney, he has averaged nearly 23 points and 11 rebounds per game. Included in that total is an incredible 39-point performance over the University of Virginia and their 7-foot, 4-inch star, Ralph Sampson. None of your starters seems to match Wood's quickness.

Sam Perkins has been an unexpected addition to the Tar Heel cause. Although only a freshman, the 6-foot, 9-inch center has held his own in contests with the famous Sampson. A cool, relaxed player, Perkins has a senior's poise to go with his 15.1 scoring average. In this game he already has seven points.

Al Wood    Sam Perkins    James Worthy

James Worthy may have more potential than either of the others. Worthy, a sophomore, chipped in with 14.6 points per game and led the team in rebounding. With great speed for a man who is 6 feet, 9 inches tall, Worthy is especially difficult for most power forwards to stay with.

The Tar Heels' backcourt, however, falls far short of their larger players. Mike Pepper and Jimmy Black scored fewer points combined than any single front liner. Matt Doherty brings a scoring touch off the bench, but at 6 feet, 7 inches, he is more suited to backing up the big guys than moving in at guard.

Jimmy Black

Mike Pepper

Matt Doherty

Your Indiana team has been admired for its man-to-man defense.

It took some time for your players to catch on to your entire system, but they have hit their peak at the right time. In the second half of their semifinal match against Louisiana State, they completely destroyed a highly regarded offense, 67-49. Your Hoosiers do not experiment with defenses; each player guards one opponent, and he had better do it well. Unfortunately, that kind of defense doesn't work when playing a group that is much better than you. So far, North Carolina's front line seems to have a big edge.

Playmaking guard Isaiah Thomas usually manages to find a way around his taller opponents.

In contrast to North Carolina, your Hoosiers lean heavily on the guards to come up with points. Your best player is the smallest man on the court, 6-foot, 1-inch Isaiah Thomas. He directs the offense, passes well, drives well, and has led the team with a 15.9 scoring average. The other guard, Randy Wittman, is a 6-foot, 6-inch bull's-eye shooter. With a three-inch height advantage over the tallest North Carolina guard, he should have no trouble getting off his shots.

Randy Wittman can score from almost anywhere on the court; under the basket he's unstoppable.

Your inside game depends on 6-foot, 9-inch senior center Ray Tolbert and 6-foot, 10-inch junior forward Landon Turner. Tolbert averaged 12.6 points and 6.3 rebounds and played nearly flawless defense. He has done even better since Turner came on strong late in the year to help out against the opposition's big men. The weak link may be 6-foot, 8-inch forward Ted Kitchell, a hard worker and good shooter who doesn't have the natural ability of most starters.

Ray Tolbert

Landon Turner

The sixth man on your team is burly 6-foot, 3-inch guard Jim Thomas. Although not much of a scorer, he is a good ball-handler, defender, and all-purpose player who led your team in rebounds against LSU with nine.

What's Your Decision?

You are the coach.
With only eight points in 10 minutes, your team would hate to sacrifice Kitchell's offense. Yet your defensive matchups do not seem to be working.
What will you do?

#1 Stay with your lineup and hope that your defense will begin to work as it did in the second half against LSU.

#2 Make an exception to your normal style of play by using a zone defense.

#3 Bring in Jim Thomas at forward to replace Kitchell.

#4 Bring in Thomas at guard and move the taller Wittman to forward.

Choose the defense. Then turn the page to find out which defense the Indiana coach chose.

Indiana chose option #3.

Although Jim Thomas was a guard, he was asked to move to forward to defend against Al Wood. The 6-foot, 3-inch Thomas would present a far quicker opponent than Wood was used to facing. Because Thomas was a powerfully built, all-around athlete, Wood was not likely to outmuscle him despite his three-inch height advantage.

If Wittman were placed at forward (#4), he could match Wood's height. But he is basically a shooter and is not likely to help your defense up front any more than Kitchell did. As for zone defenses (#2), Indiana simply did not believe in using them and preferred to juggle the lineup to get the best man-to-man matches.

Interestingly, when the Hoosiers went on offense, Wittman would change places with Thomas. His accurate shooting from the outside could draw the Tar Heel big men away from the basket.

Here's What Happened!

Indiana's new lineup seemed to put the brakes on the Tar Heel runaway victory. North Carolina had problems adjusting to the changes and managed only 10 points the rest of the first half. With Wittman sinking four straight baskets from long range, Indiana moved into a 27-26 halftime lead.

Nothing that North Carolina talked about at halftime did anything to solve the Hoosiers' new defensive pressure. Indiana stormed into a 39-30 lead early in the second half and kept the Tar Heels off stride for the rest of the game. Jim Thomas contributed far more than his two points and four rebounds would indicate. His clever passing set up teammates for eight baskets. He and Turner clamped down so well on their men that Perkins and Wood combined for a total of only five baskets and five rebounds in the entire second half. Tolbert threw a defensive blanket around Worthy who managed only seven points. North Carolina's ace players were cut down to size as they totaled only 36 points. The frustrated Tar Heels lost, 63-50, scoring fewer points than any team in an NCAA title game since 1949.

An acrobatic Isaiah Thomas (11) led Indiana with 23 points and was named MVP in the NCAA championship game.

10 The Phi Slamma Jamma Talent Show

Slamming and jamming are techniques the 1982-83 Houston Cougars have learned to perfection. Here Akeem Olajuwon (left) and Michael Young show their skill.

You are coaching the University of Houston Cougars.

You are in charge of one of the most awesome collections of athletes ever to step on a college court. During the 1982-83 season, your flashy Cougars have raced to a 31-2 record, and even that mark doesn't tell half the story. This group earned the nickname Phi Slamma Jamma in recognition of their brutal dunking clinics. In a breathtaking semi-final show, your skywalking Cougars ended the University of Louisville's claim as the dunkmasters of college basketball. Spectators cringed as Houston fired in 13 slam dunks in a 94-81 victory over the Cardinals.

In this final game against North Carolina State, your players have not been as free to show their stuff. Stifled by the slow, deliberate play of the underdog Wolfpack, your team trailed 33-25 at halftime and recorded only one dunk. But your team finally broke loose early in the second half for one of their electrifying displays, and they outscored North Carolina State by 15 points. There are nine minutes to go in the game, which you now lead, 42-35. How will you make certain that your lead holds up?

93

Consider your unlikely opponent.

North Carolina was lucky to find a spot in the tournament field. The Wolfpack sported an unimpressive 19-10 mark, and no team losing that many games has ever won an NCAA basketball title. There are only two reasons why they have made it this far. First, they have the nerves of a team of cliff divers. Secondly, they are riding a ridiculous streak of luck. Most of their tournament games have been decided in the final seconds. With 24 seconds left, the Wolfpack trailed Pepperdine by six points, and they still won. Against the Virginia Cavaliers, they overcame Virginia's last-minute lead to win the regional final.

The Wolfpack is far from helpless, though, especially at the guard positions. Husky playmaker Sidney Lowe provides steady leadership and ball control. His high school teammate, Derrick Whittenburg, has come back from an early-season injury to take over many of the scoring chores. Whittenburg will shoot from anywhere on the court.

North Carolina State is vastly outmanned under the basket, however. They do have a fine power forward, 6-foot, 11-inch Thurl Bailey, who surprised the Cougars by tossing in 15 first-half points. Bailey does not have much help, though, and the Cougars have finally gotten wise to him. The big forward has barely touched the ball in this half. The Wolfpack's other big men, 6-foot, 9-inch Lorenzo Charles and 6-foot, 10-inch Cozell McQueen, may be tall but are only good for about two baskets each per game.

Sidney Lowe

Thurl Bailey

The Wolfpack relies on Dereck Whittenburg for points.

Realizing that they don't have the raw talent of your Cougars, North Carolina State has played a slow, patient game and has avoided getting into a running game. The slow game works best when you have a lead, though, and the lead now belongs to Houston. The Wolfpack is fading, having made only 1 of their last 13 shots.

Lorenzo Charles and Cozell McQueen are two of the Wolfpack's tall men.

By contrast, your team is filled with superstars.

The Cougars have beaten their opponents by an average of over 18 points per game. National Basketball Association scouts suggest that four of the five starters are certain to be first-round pro draft choices.

The hottest Cougar in the tournament has been Akeem Abdul Olajuwon. The seven-footer from Nigeria showed up on the Houston campus one day, wanting to try out for the team. There were a few snickers at first, but Akeem has made stunning progress after a slow start. Despite his size, he has cat-like reflexes. He loves to block shots and slam home dunks, and he has been doing both at an alarming rate in the tournament. After Akeem scored 21 points, took 22 rebounds, and blocked 8 shots against Louisville, rival coaches described him as "awesome."

The only senior on the team, 6-foot, 9-inch Larry Micheaux, sometimes responds to the nickname Mr. Mean. This refers to his bruising work under the backboards. Along with Olajuwon, Micheaux makes the free-throw lane unsafe for rival visitors. The other forward is flashy Clyde Drexler. With his airborne moves, the 6-foot, 7-inch forward has been compared to Julius Erving.

To give an example of the Houston muscle, 6-foot, 6-inch guard Michael Young is even stronger than Olajuwon or Micheaux! Young has developed a nice medium-range jump shot to go with his 220 pounds and is the Cougars' leading scorer.

North Carolina State's Cozell McQueen (45) battles Akeem Abdul Olajuwon (right) and Larry Micheaux, both of Houston, during game action.

Freshman Alvin Franklin has taken over as the fifth starter and is most responsible for seeing to it that the ball gets to the four other starters. You also have a wealth of hidden talent on the bench with such athletes as guard Reid Gettys and forward Benny Anders.

The Cougars do have one glaring weakness, though. In tournament play, their weak 61 percent mark from the line has dipped to 57 percent. Oddly, Houston shoots almost as well under defensive pressure (53 percent) as they do unbothered from the foul line.

What's Your Decision?

You are the coach.
It's time to give your center, Olajuwon, a rest before the thin air at Albuquerque, New Mexico, takes a further toll on him.
What is your plan for the remaining nine minutes?

#1 Slow the game down, spread out your offense, and look for easy lay-ups.

#2 Force the pace with aggressive defense and offense.

Choose your plan. Then turn the page to find out which play the Houston coach chose.

Houston put plan #1 into action.

Of the two strategies, the first is probably the more widely used among college coaches in this situation. College teams are not required to shoot the ball within any given period of time. This puts the burden on the defense to try and get the ball back. The team with the lead usually prefers that few shots be taken because the fewer shots you take, the fewer times the opponent gets the chance to score.

Here's What Happened!

Houston's strategy played right into the hands of North Carolina State. Wolfpack coach Jim Valvano had said before the game that the tempo of the game would be crucial. If it turned into a high-scoring contest, Houston would win easily. If it was slowed to a low-scoring contest, the Wolfpack had a chance.

Houston's slowdown gave North Carolina State a chance to regroup. They were able to get back their concentration and their shots started to connect. The slowdown also tied up the Cougars' marvelous talent by having them play a less comfortable style.

With Houston holding back on offense, North Carolina State began to foul them deliberately. That forced the Cougars to protect their lead at the free-throw line. Houston missed several key free throws down the stretch that enabled the Wolfpack to catch up in the final two minutes. With the score tied at 52-52, Houston continued to play cautiously.

North Carolina continued to put the Cougars on the free-throw line as they fouled the freshman, Franklin, with 1:05 left in the game. Franklin had to make the first free throw to get a chance to shoot a second one, but he missed.

North Carolina State rebounded and set up for a game-winning play. Houston's defense was up to the task, though, and forced Whittenburg to launch a hopeless shot from 35 feet away with only a few seconds left. The ball didn't even make it to the rim, but the Wolfpack's Lorenzo Charles happened to be standing all alone near the basket. He pulled the ball out of the air and soared high to dunk it for the winning points. With an assist from the Houston strategy, North Carolina State wound up as the NCAA's 1983 basketball champion.

Dereck Whittenburg launches the last-second shot...

...that Lorenzo Charles slam dunks to spoil Houston's Phi Slamma Jamma show.

ACKNOWLEDGMENTS

Photo credits: p. 78, Duke University; pp. 86, 87, 88, Indiana University; pp. 21, 22, Marquette University; pp. 36, 40, 41, 45, 95, 96, North Carolina State University; p. 29, Seattle University; p. 4, Phil Steinberg; pp. 10, 11, 39, 62, UCLA; pp. 7, 9, 30, 55, 56, 103, United Press International; p. 92, University of Houston; pp. 59, 61, University of Louisville; pp. 84, 85, University of North Carolina; p. 18, University of North Carolina-Charlotte; pp. 46, 50, 51, 52, University of Texas-El Paso; pp. 17, 26, 35, 49, 65, 66, 70, 73, 74, 77, 81, 82, 91, 98, 101, 102, Wide World Photos.

Cover photograph: Rich Clarkson/SPORTS ILLUSTRATED.

Also by Nate Aaseng

BASEBALL: IT'S YOUR TEAM
10 do-or-die dilemmas

FOOTBALL: IT'S YOUR TEAM
10 sink-or-swim situations

BASEBALL: YOU ARE THE MANAGER
10 exciting championship games

BASKETBALL: YOU ARE THE COACH
10 exciting NBA play-off games

FOOTBALL: YOU ARE THE COACH
10 exciting NFL play-off games

HOCKEY: YOU ARE THE COACH
10 exciting NHL play-off and international games

COLLEGE FOOTBALL: YOU ARE THE COACH
10 exciting bowl games

Lerner Publications Company
241 First Avenue North, Minneapolis, MN 55401